KU-099-406

The Making of a Champion

A World-Class
Marathon Runner

Haydn Middleton

www.heinemann.co.uk/library
Visit our website to find out more information about **Heinemann Library** books.

To order:
☎ Phone 44 (0) 1865 888066
🖹 Send a fax to 44 (0) 1865 314091
💻 Visit the Heinemann Bookshop at www.heinemann.co.uk/library to browse our catalogue and order online.

First published in Great Britain by Heinemann Library, Halley Court, Jordan Hill, Oxford OX2 8EJ, part of Harcourt Education. Heinemann is a registered trademark of Harcourt Education Ltd.

© Harcourt Education Ltd 2004
The moral right of the proprietor has been asserted.

Editorial: Andrew Farrow and Dan Nunn
Design: David Poole and Geoff Ward
Illustrations: Geoff Ward
Picture Research: Rebecca Sodergren and Fiona Orbell
Production: Viv Hichens

Originated by Ambassador Litho Ltd
Printed in China by WKT Company Limited

ISBN 0 431 18923 4
08 07 06 05 04
10 9 8 7 6 5 4 3 2 1

British Library Cataloguing in Publication Data
Middleton, Haydn
A World-Class Marathon Runner - (The Making of a Champion)
1. Marathon running - Juvenile literature
2. Marathon running - Training - Juvenile literature
I. Title
796.4'252
A full catalogue record for this book is available from the British Library.

Acknowledgements
The publishers would like to thank the following for permission to reproduce photographs:

Action Plus pp. **5 top** (Glyn Kirk), **13 left**, **23 bottom**, **42** (Glyn Kirk); Associated Press pp. **9 top**, **25 top**, **25 bottom**, **29**, **37 bottom**, **39 bottom**; Corbis pp. **4** (Hulton-Deutsch Collection), **6** (Gianni Dagli Orti), **10** (Bettmann), **14 right** (David Stoecklein), **16** (Kit Little), **18** (Yann Arthus-Bertrand), **22** (S. Carmona), **40** (Bohemian Nomad Picturemakers), **43 top** (Bettmann), **43 bottom** (Bettmann); Empics pp. **12** (Matthew Ashton), **19** (DPA), **27 top** (Matthew Ashton), **28** (Steve Etherington), **35 right** (S&G/Alpha); L'Equipe pp. **15**, **37 top**; Getty Images pp. **7 top**, **9 bottom**, **13 right**, **14 left**, **17** (All Sport), **20**, **21**, **24**, **31 bottom** (All Sport), **38**; Getty News and Sport p. **36 top** (All Sport/Tony Duffy); Hulton Archive p. **7 bottom**; New York Road Runners p. **30**; PA Photos pp. **5 bottom** (Tom Hevezi), **11 top** (John Stillwell), **11 bottom** (Abaca Press), **41** (Michael Crabtree); Reuters pp. **33** (Peter MacDiarmid), **34** (Gary Hershorn), **35 left**, **39 top** (Jerry Lampen); Richard Nerurkar p. **27 bottom**; Runningtimes.com p. **31 top**; Sporting Pictures p. **23 top**.

Cover photograph reproduced with permission of PA Photos.

Every effort has been made to contact copyright holders of any material reproduced in this book. Any omissions will be rectified in subsequent printings if notice is given to the publishers.

This book is dedicated to the memory of the great Czech athlete Emil Zátopek (1922–2000), who ran his first-ever marathon at the 1952 Olympic Games in Helsinki, Finland. He won, setting a new Olympic record time, and so added a third gold medal to those he had already won in the 5000m and 10,000m.

Contents

Words printed in bold letters, **like these**, are explained in the Glossary.

In this book, each athlete's time for completing the marathon is shown as follows: first hours, then minutes, then seconds, e.g. '2:23:03.2'. This means that the time was 2 hours, 23 minutes and 3.2 seconds.

The ultimate challenge

People use the word 'marathon' a lot today. It describes anything that takes a long time and is quite hard to get through: a marathon meal, a marathon film. Until just over a hundred years ago, the word was virtually unknown. That was when the true marathon was invented – a long-distance foot race that took a *very* long time and was very hard to complete. The marathon was the ultimate sporting challenge – and it still is. Anyone who sets out to complete a course of 42.195 km (26 miles and 385 yards) is aiming high. Anyone who wins such a race is a true champion.

Being prepared

The marathon is a unique event. More than 30,000 runners can take part in a single race, and first-time runners can compete alongside reigning Olympic champions – at least for the first few metres! They must all be fully prepared for the great test ahead. For weeks and months, they will have eaten right, drunk right, slept right, trained right and rested right. By the time they hear the starting pistol they should be at the peak of physical fitness.

Thinking on your feet

Marathon runners have to prepare mentally, too. Whereas a 100m sprint can last less than 10 seconds, a marathon goes on for over 2 hours. That is a long time for even the best runners to concentrate – not just on their own performance, but also on what is happening around them. They need to make sure they are not running too fast or too slowly at any time. It is important that they stick to the pace that they know is best for them.

At the London Olympic Games of 1908 an exhausted Italian, Dorando Pietri, was the first runner to reach the stadium, where most Olympic marathons end. But Pietri needed help to stagger across the finishing line, so he had to be disqualified from the race.

Mind games

Marathon-running – it is said – is like playing chess on your feet. 'There are so many mind games being played,' says champion runner Paula Radcliffe. 'Sometimes [during a race] you'll offer an athlete a drink just to show you have the energy to do so. Other times you might not, just because you think it will make her think you're weak [and so she will underestimate you]… There are a million ways to run a marathon and it's all about getting the better of your opponents.'

Other champions, however, believe the biggest contest of all is with the race itself – with those gruelling 42.195 km. 'You may be in the same race as three or 30,000 others,' writes Richard Nerurkar, a British marathon star of the 1990s, 'but really the contest is between you and the distance.'

At the Atlanta, USA, Games of 1996, Josiah Thugwane of South Africa won the closest-ever Olympic marathon. He was the victor by just 3 seconds! He is pictured here crossing the finishing line.

Khalid Khannouchi of the USA wins the 2002 London Marathon in a new world-record time of 2:05:38 – breaking his own world record.

How marathons began

People have raced since ancient times. From 776 BC until AD 393, athletes from all over ancient Greece came to a place called Olympia every four years to compete against one another. At these 'Olympic' Games there was no marathon. The longest foot race was over a distance of around 4000–5000 metres. But although no marathon was run at the ancient Olympics, the name 'marathon' does come from ancient Greece.

Pheidippides shows the way

Marathon is the name of a place on Greece's east coast. In 490 BC, an invading Persian army landed there. According to legend, the Greeks in that area sent a runner to the Greek state of Sparta – about 240 km away – to seek help to drive off the Persians. His name was Pheidippides. The battle took place before Spartan soldiers could arrive – yet the local Greeks still won.

Following this success, the Greeks once more sent a runner from the battlefield at Marathon, this time to run the roughly 40 km to the Greek state of Athens, carrying news of the victory. Historians say that after delivering his message of 'Rejoice, we conquer', the messenger collapsed and died. Since he was still wearing his armour, the cause was probably heat exhaustion!

The ancient Greeks took athletics very seriously. Their greatest athletic heroes were not just highly skilful, they were also expected to perform fairly, gracefully, and even beautifully.

Going the distance

The first modern marathon races, around the year 1900, were run over a distance of roughly 40 km too. This was in honour of the distance covered by the runner from Marathon. (On page 8 you can find out how the distance of 42.195 km became fixed.) During the 19th century, organized sport with rules and regulations had become very popular in Europe and America. Long-distance racing was especially popular in France. In 1885, for example, there was a 38 km race from Paris to Versailles, won by Louis Saussus in a time of 2:26:30. It was a Frenchman too, Pierre de Coubertin, who had the idea of re-starting the Olympic Games as an **amateur** sporting festival for athletes from all over the world. The official history of the marathon was about to begin...

Runners in the 2002 Athens marathon pass a statue of the very first marathon runner, Pheidippides.

In the late 19th century, before the first marathons took place, large crowds turned out to watch international six-day-long walking races like this one in New York City.

'Ped' fact

'Pedestrianism' was a popular 19th-century **professional** sport. In the UK and the USA athletes called 'Peds' walked or ran against each other, or in races against the clock. They bet money on who would win; so did huge crowds of spectators. Some of the events lasted for days. In 1809 Captain Barclay Allardice successfully walked 1000 miles (1609 km) in 1000 hours on the heath at Newmarket, England, for a bet of 1000 **guineas**.

The Olympic marathon

The first international Olympic Games were held in Athens, Greece in 1896. A marathon race was staged between Marathon itself and the Panathinaikon Stadium in Athens. It was a tough course – one of only four Olympic Games courses that was, overall, more uphill than downhill. A local runner finished first (see panel on page 9). Another Greek finished third but was later disqualified – officials found he had ridden part of the way in a carriage!

Fixing the distance

Since 1896, Olympic Games have been held every four years (except during the two world wars). But until the Paris Games of 1924 there was no fixed distance for the marathon. Courses varied in length from 40 km to 42.75 km. This made it hard to compare the times athletes took to complete races. So in 1924, the International **Amateur** Athletic Federation (IAAF) set the official Olympic distance at 42.195 km.

That was the length of the course in London's 1908 Games. Surviving records do not explain why this distance was chosen, but it became the standard.

This was the route of the 1908 Olympic marathon held in London. Its original distance was 26 miles – but then organizers added an extra 385 yards inside the stadium. This meant that the race could finish directly in front of Queen Alexandra's seat!

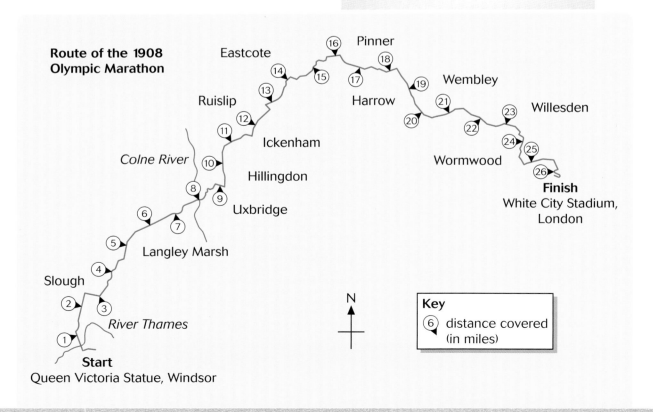

Route of the 1908 Olympic Marathon

Pinner
Eastcote
Wembley
Ruislip
Harrow
Willesden
Ickenham
Colne River
Hillingdon
Wormwood
Uxbridge
Finish
White City Stadium, London
Langley Marsh
Slough
River Thames
Start
Queen Victoria Statue, Windsor

N

Key
6 distance covered (in miles)

Late start for women

The first woman to be officially timed in a marathon run was the UK's Violet Piercey in 1926. She completed the course in 3:40:22. Her 'record' stood for 37 years, until the USA's Merry Lepper ran 3:37:07 in 1963. Eight years later, Australian Adrienne Beames became the first woman to run a marathon in under 3 hours, and in 1983 the USA's Joan Benoit brought the women's world record down to 2:22:43. Yet women were still not allowed to race in an Olympic marathon.

This was because some sports organizers, and some doctors, believed women's bodies could not meet the demands of such long-distance running. There was not even a 1500m event for women until the 1972 Games. Finally, at the 1984 Games in Los Angeles, female distance runners got what they had been campaigning for: an Olympic marathon. Joan Benoit won that first race in a time of 2:24:52 – faster than 13 of the 20 previous male Olympic champions!

A scene from the first Olympic marathon for women, staged at the Los Angeles Games of 1984. Many spectators wept with emotion to see women athletes finally being allowed to compete in the most demanding of all races.

The original Olympic champion

Greek **labourer** Spiridon Louis won the first Olympic marathon in 1896, aged 23. His finishing time was 2:58:50, more than 7 minutes faster than the second-placed runner. Although he was offered many gifts for winning, he accepted only a horse and cart to help transport water to his village of Amaroussion, near Athens. Louis had no proper athletic training, and after his victory never competed again, but he was a guest of honour at the 1936 Berlin Olympics. He died in 1940 and is buried at Amaroussion, the site for a magnificent Olympic stadium for the 2004 Games.

City marathons

The first Olympic marathon of 1896 started a trend. Later that same year the first US marathon was staged between Stamford, Connecticut and New York City. Then, in April 1897, fifteen runners competed in a Boston Athletic Association Marathon from Ashland into the city of Boston itself. The Boston Marathon became an annual, international event. So many runners wanted to take part that by 1970 its organizers had to set a **qualifying time**. In 1996 it was run for the 100th year in a row – making it the world's oldest continuously held marathon. And during those 100 years, the number of competitors rose from just 15 to 38,000!

London Marathon fact

A key founder of the London Marathon was journalist and ex-Olympic **steeplechase** champion Chris Brasher (1928–2003). In 1979, aged 51, he ran in the New York City Marathon. That gave him the idea to try to launch a marathon in London. He succeeded two years later.

A bird's-eye view of thousands of runners competing in the 1982 New York City Marathon. (One of the main jobs of city marathon organizers is to keep the streets clear of traffic!)

'People's marathons'

Many big cities now close down for a day to stage marathons. They are marvellous to run in or to watch from the sidelines or on TV, but they take a lot of organizing! The first New York City Marathon in 1970 had just 55 finishers, and was staged with a budget of just $1000. Today its 30,000 runners are supported by 12,000 volunteer helpers, dozens of sponsors and many city departments.

Even harder to organize is the London Marathon. Since 1981 over half a million competitors have crossed the finishing line near Buckingham Palace. These range from world-record holders and other **elite** international athletes to keep-fit enthusiasts, wheelchair racers, and even veterans over 80 years old. Every year, **sponsored runners** in the London Marathon raise enormous sums of money for charity, too; in 2002 they brought in £31 million.

For runners and spectators alike, city marathons can be huge fun. This runner competed in the 2002 New York City Marathon wearing a deep-sea diver's suit. His finishing time was 5 days, 3 hours, 20 minutes and 23 seconds!

Armchair fan to wheelchair champ!

Tanni Grey-Thompson was born in Wales in 1969, disabled by **spina bifida**. As a girl she came to rely on a wheelchair, but grew to love sport too. Inspired by watching the London Marathon on TV, she became a wheelchair athlete. At the age of eighteen she took part in her first international competition. Since then she has become one of the world's most successful and popular disabled athletes. Her feats include winning the wheelchair division of the London Marathon six times. She won the race in 2002 just two months after giving birth!

Preparing to run a marathon

You could decide to become a marathon runner and then complete a 42.195 km race the very next day. You would, however, need to be amazingly fit and healthy to do so. Most people are not naturally able to run so far. So both **elite** athletes and runners-for-fun spend a long period building up to the big race. Some of that time is used for specialist training. But, as you will see, race-preparation involves more than simply applying to run in a marathon, then running practice kilometres.

Living the marathon life

Respected marathon runner and writer Hal Higdon lists five goals for the successful marathoner:

- follow a proper diet
- work to reduce any flabbiness in the body
- do not smoke, or drink too much alcohol
- get enough sleep
- exercise regularly.

This can mean altering the way you live your life, making you much fitter along the way. Marathons can thus make you healthier, although people who have medical problems already are advised not to take up the marathon challenge. There are also regulations in most countries against people under the age of eighteen competing. Young people can, however, prepare their growing bodies for the marathon by running long-distance track events, or competing in cross-country races.

Italian athlete Stefano Baldini here shows an extremely efficient running posture. The best marathon runners use a short, quick stride with a relatively low knee lift. They also keep their heads and shoulders relaxed, even as the rest of their bodies grow tired.

Grete the Great!

So many people want to run in city marathons that some inexperienced runners are turned down. In 1978 the New York Road Runners Club rejected Grete Waitz (right) of Norway because she had never run more than 12 miles (19.3 km) before. But since she had a good record at shorter distances, the Club then decided to let her run – just to set the pace for others. Grete went on to win the race in a world record time of 2:32:29.8! Before retiring in 1990, she won the race nine times, also picking up a silver medal at the 1984 Olympics.

Cushioned shoes help to soften the impact of running long distances on hard surfaces. But shoes that are too spongy offer little support to the foot, and can be a cause of injuries. Depending on wear and tear, a pair of shoes can last a runner for up to 1600 km.

Medical fact

At the first women's Olympic marathon in 1984, Gabriele Andersen-Scheiss of Switzerland finished 37th. She had become so ill, however, that it took her 5 minutes and 44 seconds to stagger around the last lap of the track. Doctors hovered nearby, but the runner waved them away. She knew the rule: if they gave her any medical help, she would be disqualified. After the race, the IAAF passed the 'Scheiss Rule'. A runner can now have an in-race medical exam and not be disqualified. But if the doctors think the runner is unfit to continue, he or she must retire from the race.

Training goals and patterns

There are many different ways to run a marathon, but there are probably even more ways to train for one. In the period leading up to a marathon, each athlete follows a varied, highly personal training pattern. How do they plan such a pattern? 'There are two ways to learn about training,' according to sports medicine specialist Dr Stan James of Oregon, USA. 'One is by having access to a very knowledgeable coach. The other is by trial and error.'

Old goal, new success

When Paula Radcliffe was eleven, her father Peter ran the London Marathon. Her goal was to run it with him one day. He encouraged her to run cross-country (in one of her first races she finished 299th!), then as she grew older she became an international long-distance track runner. In 2002 she returned to her first goal, although her father no longer ran. She won the London Marathon – her first race at the distance – and then broke the world record at the Chicago Marathon. Here you see her in training before the 2002 London Marathon.

Since running long distance can be a lonely business, it can help to run with a friend or a training partner. This athlete is combining training with child care!

Breaking the year into periods

If an athlete's main race of the year is in April – like the London Marathon – he or she can plan to make it the goal of a year-long training pattern. This year can be broken down into periods, each with its own type of training and goal. Below is an example.

If this 'periodization' works well for an athlete, he or she can do the same thing the following year. Sometimes, however, it helps to work out a new pattern with a coach. Fresh challenges keep training interesting.

Timetable	Type of training	Reason or major goal
May–July	Faster running over shorter distances. Do some track work.	Preparation for running in 5 km and 10 km races
Early August	Low level of training	Enjoy a break from training routine
Late August–September	Increase **mileage** and use 10-km and 10-mile races to build fitness	Preparation for half-marathon race in October
November–December	Keep up some long runs, but reduce overall mileage. Include running up hills.	Preparation for cross-country races
Late December	Low level of training over Christmas	Chance to let body relax a little
January–March	Period of hardest training in build-up to race day	Preparation for running marathon in April
April–May	Reduce training in days leading up to the race	Let muscles recover from training. Race well, then rest well.

Runners can train in the most exotic locations! Amateur and professional athletes alike often make use of training camps abroad. There, in the company of other athletes, coaches and doctors, they can learn from one another as they follow their training routines.

Fuelling the body

The marathon at the 1912 Olympics in Stockholm ended in tragedy. Francisco Lazaro, a runner from Portugal, collapsed with sunstroke and heart trouble. He was rushed to hospital, but he died the next day. Marathon running puts a huge strain on the human body. Doctors today can give expert advice on how to prepare for races. **Nutritionists** too can advise on how to keep up energy levels during training.

Eating for energy

Energy comes from food. About 70 per cent of the energy obtained from food makes the body work; it makes sure the heart keeps pumping and so on. The remaining 30 per cent can be used for activities like running. The amount of energy provided by foods depends on how much water, **protein**, fat and **carbohydrates** they contain.

The best foods for distance runners are high in carbohydrates – such as pasta, bread, vegetables like potatoes, and certain cereals and fruits like bananas. 'Carbs' are easy to digest, and easy to turn into energy-giving glucose (a form of sugar that circulates in the blood) and **glycogen**, which is a vital source of energy for the liver and muscles. But after about 32 km of a marathon, an athlete's glycogen store can run out. At this stage of the race, runners can feel so tired that they call it 'hitting the wall'. They then have to rely more on their body fat for energy. By running long distances regularly, marathoners train their bodies to use both sources of energy more efficiently.

Since 1984, the IAAF has allowed runners to be medically examined during a race without being disqualified (see page 13). However, the race looks over for this athlete.

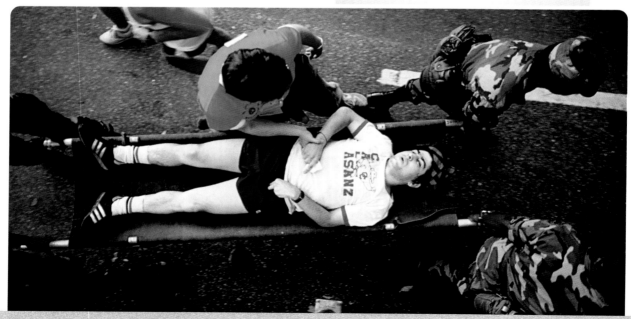

As well as carbs, marathon runners need some fats to help repair muscles, and some proteins to help the body recover after training. They do not have to worry too much about the exact amounts, as long as their overall diet is healthy. Runners do, however, need to eat a lot of food, since they burn off so many **calories** with all their exercise. (People lose about 100 calories for every mile they walk or run. But, interestingly, they need to use around 3500 calories in order to lose just one pound in weight.)

The body takes in fats, carbohydrates and proteins from food. Chemicals in the body, plus oxygen, turn the food into energy. Waste products, such as carbon dioxide and water, are also produced.

Fats → Carbohydrates → Proteins
→ Glucose
Oxygen → Intermediate chemicals
Water ← Energy → Carbon dioxide

Drugs fact

Some ways of fuelling the body for a marathon are not allowed. The International Olympic Committee publishes a list of banned drugs. These drugs can cause harm, or give athletes an unfair advantage in races. Marathon runners are forbidden to use 'stimulants' that reduce tiredness; 'narcotics' that act on the brain to reduce pain; 'anabolic agents' that affect muscle size; and 'hormone substances' that can increase strength. Also forbidden are 'diuretics', which can be used to disguise other drugs in the body.

A dope-test being carried out on an athlete's urine sample. Tests are taken during marathon training as well as at races. The first Olympic marathon runner to be disqualified for drug abuse was the Russian Madina Biktagirova in 1992.

Building strength and endurance

A person's body is a very complicated thing. The heart, blood vessels, lungs and **circulatory system** all have to work together. How well they work together depends on how fit the person is. Marathon runners must be ultra-fit, so they work on building up their strength and endurance. In their training programmes they gradually exercise their hearts and lungs harder, to make them work more efficiently.

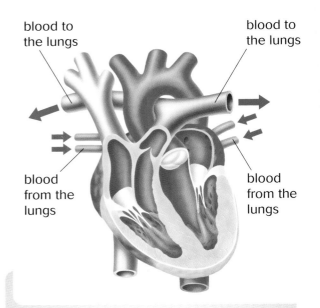

blood to the lungs

blood to the lungs

blood from the lungs

blood from the lungs

This is a cross-section of the human heart – the organ that pumps blood to and from the lungs, where the oxygen needed to produce energy is collected.

Some marathon runners like to work with weights and exercise machines. Strength training adds variety to their schedules, and can be important for conditioning the body and helping to prevent injury.

Making the body work better

Marathon running is an 'aerobic' activity. This means runners use oxygen to produce the energy they need. First they breathe in oxygen from the air. Then the oxygen is taken into the blood, and carried to the muscles. Trained runners can inhale three litres of air with a single breath. Untrained people can manage only about two.

Careful training thickens and strengthens the muscle **fibres** around the heart too. This lets the runner's heart pump more blood with each stroke. In this way, oxygen can be carried faster and more efficiently to the muscles than in untrained people.

Strong and steady

What kind of training builds strength and endurance? The answer, mainly, is running. But this running has to be done on a regular weekly basis – pushing the body too hard over too short a period can cause serious injuries. Top runners may do two workouts a day; some modern Kenyan runners – among the very best in the world – do three.

The USA's Frank Shorter, Olympic marathon champion in 1972, was an elite athlete who opted for very heavy mileage in training, to build strength and endurance. At his peak he ran 225 training km per week.

Most **elite** marathoners like to run about 160 km each week, then reduce or 'taper' this figure just before races. There can, however, be a danger of running high **mileage** just for its own sake. Athletes will not improve their fitness or performance by running extra 'junk miles'. Each person has to find his or her own most useful and comfortable mileage level, then stick to it steadily – taking care not to skip training days. Athletes who skip training run the risk of 'detraining' or losing the fitness they previously built up.

The long run

'If you feel bad after 10 miles, you're in trouble. If you feel bad at 20 miles, you're normal. If you don't feel bad at 26 miles, you're abnormal!', according to champion Australian marathoner Rob de Castella (see panel opposite). No one finds it easy to run the full marathon distance. But in order to complete the course on race day, athletes need plenty of experience at 'running long'. That is why they build regular 32-km workouts into their training programmes. Tom Grogan, a coach from Cincinnati in the USA, believes that, for top marathon runners, the long run comes second in importance only to 'raw talent'.

Practice makes perfect

Running long is a dress rehearsal for the race. It gets athletes used to the stress of lifting their feet up and down around 8000–10,000 times per hour. It offers practice at race skills, like taking fluids along the route (see page 22). It also teaches patience to those who push too hard on their daily runs.

The peak distance is usually 32 km. (Some coaches suggest their athletes run for 3 hours instead. **Elite** Japanese runners go for 5-hour runs.) Too many long runs in the build-up to a race can be harmful, though, as this makes injuries more likely, and can almost make an athlete bored with running.

Paula Radcliffe at rest in La Manga, Spain, prior to the 2002 London Marathon. Rest is vital after a long run, especially for new runners. It may take up to two weeks for them to recover fully. A bit of rest before a long run is important too, since this can make it easier for the body to recover afterwards.

How fast should long runs be?

Many coaches suggest taking long runs quite slowly. Regular fast runs are just too demanding. Some coaches even approve of 'walking breaks' along the way. For athletes, the important thing is to spend enough time on their feet. Runners who can finish marathons in under 2:10 have been known to pace their long runs at over 7 minutes per mile (that is more than 3 hours over the full marathon distance). But not every run has to be at the same pace. And some runners prefer to run the second half of a run faster than the first half.

The table below shows the recommendations of a number of top coaches on running long while building up to a big race.

Category	First timers	Experienced runners
Longest run	32 km	37 km
Frequency	1 time	3–6 times
Pace per mile	Race pace	30–90 seconds slower than race pace
Weekly distance	64 km	89–97 km
Walking breaks	Yes	No
Speedwork on route (see page 25)	No	Yes

Running longer

Australian Rob de Castella, born in 1957, firmly believed in the value of long runs. In building up to a marathon he would run 23-milers (37 km) nearly every weekend. Then he would peak with a 30-miler (48 km) five weeks before race day. His powers of endurance enabled him to compete in four Olympic marathons, from 1980 to 1992, with a best finish of fifth in 1984. Along the way, he also won the Boston Marathon of 1986 in a time of 2:07:51, and was the Commonwealth Games marathon champion in 1982 and 1986.

Fluid replacement tactics

Water makes up about 60 per cent of a person's body weight. One of the many jobs it does is to stop the body overheating. To function in a healthy way, the body has to remain at a constant temperature of 37–38 °C (98–100 °F). When someone runs, his or her muscles produce extra heat. The body copes with this rise in temperature by sweating. As water evaporates from the surface of the skin, heat is lost and the body cools down.

This runner is sweating heavily. Although this will help him to keep cool, he will need to take regular drinks of water during the race to avoid becoming dehydrated.

Dehydration

On long runs, especially in hot or **humid** weather, an athlete can sweat off up to 2 litres an hour. (In normal everyday life, through natural processes, we lose about the same amount of fluid each day.) All this lost fluid has to be replaced, or else the athlete becomes dehydrated. Dehydration during training for a race is no fun. It can lead to sickness, diarrhoea, breathing difficulties, and even, in the most severe cases, collapse from heat stroke. It is also a major cause of muscle soreness after a long period of exercise.

Battling dehydration

Marathon runners must be well **hydrated** before, during and after long runs and races. This will improve their performance as well as ensure their safety. What they drink is a matter of personal choice. As well as water, they can use sports drinks with the bubbles taken out. Some sports drinks contain special mixtures of **carbohydrates** (which give extra fuel) and 'electrolytes'. These are salty substances that already exist in the body but have to be kept topped up. Electrolytes can replace salts lost through sweating, and so make it easier for water to be absorbed.

'Water in, water on'

Like many runners, champion athlete Richard Nerurkar aims to drink 100–150 ml of fluid every 5 km throughout the race. 'Drink little and often' he suggests, even in cool conditions. By the time a runner feels thirsty, he or she is already dehydrated.

It usually takes 30 minutes for fluid to work its way through the system before being sweated out. So in the last stages of a race, just splashing water on the body can help too. As it evaporates away, it reduces the runner's body heat a little, and so has a cooling effect.

A drinks station at the end of a marathon. It is an Olympic rule that such stations should be placed every 5 km along the route, so that athletes can keep 'topping up' and so avoid dehydration.

Sweat fact

Losing 2 per cent of body weight through sweating can result in a 20 per cent drop in an athlete's **aerobic** performance. With a 5 per cent loss, the ability to train can drop by up to 33 per cent. Failure to replace fluid while distance running can also result in a thickening of the blood in the **coronary arteries**, which increases the possibility of heart attacks.

Rehydrating like this without breaking step can be difficult. Younger runners need to practise this skill, or they may risk choking.

Measuring performance

Early marathon racers did not take a very scientific approach to their event. Cuba's Felix Carvajal arrived as a hitchhiker at the 1904 Olympics in St Louis, USA. He appeared on the starting line wearing heavy street shoes, long trousers, a long-sleeved shirt and a beret. The start of the race was delayed while his trousers were cut off at the knees. During the race he raided an orchard for some apples, got an attack of stomach cramps – and still managed to finish fourth! Such a free-and-easy approach is less likely in today's highly competitive world. Marathon runners have to take their sport far more seriously – and many make use of laboratories dedicated to measuring athletic performance.

'Treadmills' can be found in most modern gyms. They are simply moving belts, on which athletes can run 'on-the-spot' while a coach or medical assistant makes various measurements. Here, boxer Frank Bruno is using a treadmill to train before competing in the London Marathon.

Oxygen for energy

A common modern measuring device is the treadmill. While athletes run flat out on-the-spot, their ability to absorb oxygen can be assessed. An athlete's Maximum Oxygen Intake Capacity (VO2 Max, for short) is a measure of the heart's capacity to pump oxygen-rich blood to the muscles, and how efficiently the muscles then use it. It is calculated from the number of millilitres of oxygen that is absorbed during 60 seconds, per kilogram of body weight.

An **elite** runner with a VO2 Max of, say, 70 should be able to run a marathon in 2:23:00. Then he or she can check whether the figure of 70 improves if they run greater distances each week. Yet runners with very high VO2 values can still be outperformed by athletes with more efficient running styles. That is why many coaches, using video cameras and computer analysis, also aim to show their athletes how to make their running action more efficient.

The value of speed

Another way to improve running form is to include **speedwork** in the training programme. This means running at a significantly faster pace than an athlete would run in an actual marathon. According to Dr Melvin H. Williams, a professor of exercise science at Old Dominion University in Virginia, USA, 'by training faster you improve specific muscles used at higher speeds... If you can run faster at short distances, you can increase your absolute ability at longer distances too.' By adding speedwork to his own training, Williams cut his own personal best time from the 2:50s to 2:33:30 at age 44 – and he did not stop to raid any orchards on the way!

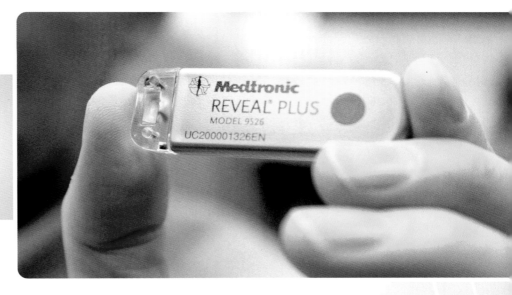

This is a heart-rate monitor. Athletes can wear them on 'recovery runs', to check that their heart-rate stays at 70–75 per cent of their usual maximum.

The small device laced into this shoe is a 1990s invention called the ChampionChip®. It automatically records the runner's precise starting time as he or she crosses an electronic carpet at the starting line. It also records the precise moments when further carpets are crossed along the route. In this way, runners can later obtain a very clear picture of their whole performance.

Injury and recovery

Marathons test the human body to the limit, so runners are bound to pick up injuries. But many doctors agree that most running injuries are the result of 'overtraining'. Athletes who set themselves tough targets often ignore the warnings that their own bodies give them. Instead of adjusting their targets (the sensible way to stay fit) they train on, even though they feel pain or weariness. In the end they train themselves past breaking point, and it can take a long time to put the damage right.

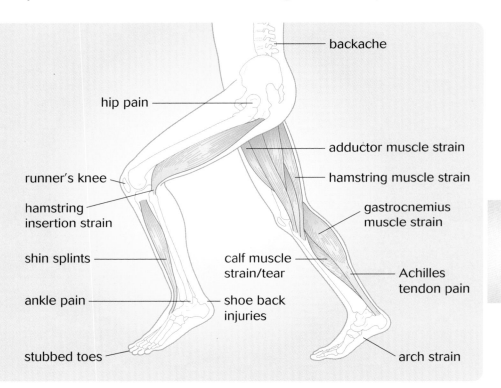

backache

hip pain

adductor muscle strain

hamstring muscle strain

runner's knee

gastrocnemius muscle strain

hamstring insertion strain

shin splints

calf muscle strain/tear

Achilles tendon pain

ankle pain

shoe back injuries

stubbed toes

arch strain

This diagram shows the main problem areas in a distance-runner's lower body.

What can go wrong?

The diagram above shows where problems can occur in the distance-runner's lower body. When leg muscles feel weak or stiff, this can affect the whole body's balance, and result in pain in the hip and lower back too. Stress fractures in the bones of the lower limbs and feet can result from over-exercise, or from small repeated movements. Ankle sprains can be caused by sudden wrenching, particularly when running on uneven ground. **Achilles tendons** can be damaged if the runner is not sufficiently warmed up or is wearing unsuitable footwear, while shin splints (sharp pain and tightness on the outside of the shin) can be caused by poor posture or by running high **mileage** on hard surfaces. For this reason, runners should train on soft surfaces as much as possible.

'Dynamic repair'

Many basic injuries can be quickly put right. But stretching and strengthening exercises, warming up before exercise and cooling down after it (see page 41), can help to prevent them in the first place. A massage 48 hours after a long run, often the peak point of muscle soreness, can also help. Best of all, athletes should build regular rest days into their training programmes. These are periods of what New York coach Bob Glover calls 'dynamic repair'.

After hard exercise, most bodies need 48 hours to recover. The purpose of training is to break down many of the body's parts, like tiny muscle **fibres**, so that they will then rebuild themselves more strongly than before. In this way, stress can create strength. But if athletes do without the vital rebuilding time after exercise, they will overtrain – and create all kinds of problems for themselves.

With some injuries, the athlete just has to grin and bear it. Days before the Olympic marathon in Atlanta, USA, in 1996, the UK's high-flying Liz McColgan suffered a painful insect bite to her foot. She still took part in the race – and came home in sixteenth place.

A long lay-off – sort of!

Some injuries need more than just rest. The UK's Richard Nerurkar (pictured here with his feet in an ice bath) won the Hamburg Marathon and World Cup Marathon in 1993. But two years later, his right foot was giving him so much pain that he had to have it checked out. A bone growth on his big toe had to be operated on. His **rehabilitation** period included six weeks of no running at all. He could, however, train in other ways – and how! Over one ten-day period his daily training consisted of a 1200-metre swim, 45 minutes of running in the pool, a 60-mile (97-km) bike ride, 30 minutes of gym work, and some gentle walking!

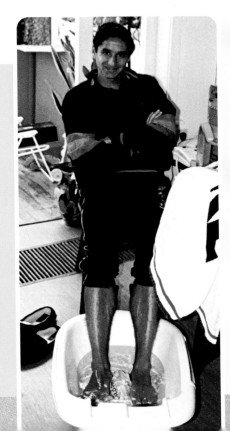

Knowing the course

The 1900 Olympic Games were held in Paris, France. The marathon winner there was Michel Théato of Luxembourg, who lived and worked in the city. According to reports, he was a deliveryman for a bakery. Some American runners accused him of using his knowledge of Paris's streets to take a few short cuts during the race! This may not have been true, but driving over the course in advance is usually a big help to marathon runners. (To marathon runner Hal Higdon, however, 'the hills always seem steeper and the miles longer when you're riding over them rather than running'!)

Tricky terrain

At the 1992 Olympics in Barcelona, Spain, the marathon race ended with an awesomely steep climb up the hill of Montjuïc (see picture). After approaching the 35 km mark at sea level, the runners had to finish in the Olympic Stadium which was 97 metres above. That sudden final ascent would have come as an unpleasant surprise to an unprepared athlete!

All marathon courses are different. That is a great attraction of the event. It is also a great challenge. Large parts of the Boston Marathon are run downhill; this means athletes can run the course fast, but many practise running down slopes before the race to prepare the big muscles at the front of their thighs for the strain.

This is Montjuïc, the hill or 'mountain' in Barcelona, Spain, which Olympic marathon runners in 1992 had to climb in the race's final stages!

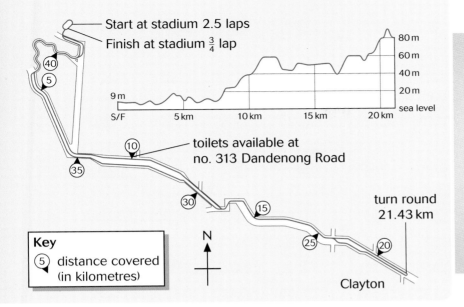

Start at stadium 2.5 laps
Finish at stadium ¾ lap

9 m

S/F   5 km   10 km   15 km   20 km

80 m
60 m
40 m
20 m
sea level

40
5

10   toilets available at
      no. 313 Dandenong Road

35

30

15

25   20

turn round
21.43 km

N

Clayton

Key
5   distance covered
     (in kilometres)

This was the route of the 1956 Olympic marathon in Melbourne, Australia. The runners ran just over 20 km in one direction, then ran back to the starting point. A broken green line was painted on the streets, showing the runners which way to go. (Notice how places are marked for toilet-breaks in an emergency!)

Getting to know the climate

Athletes have to take into account the climate at a course too. Several early Olympic marathons took place in sweltering heat, which had a bad effect on many runners. The 1960 Olympic marathon in Rome was the first to be held in the evening, when temperatures were sure to be cooler. The 1968 Olympics were held in high-altitude Mexico City. A year before that, to help runners from countries nearer sea level to get used to the conditions, the organizers staged an international race over the Olympic marathon course. As a result, in the actual race of 1968, only two of the top ten finishers (both Ethiopians) came from another high-altitude country with a climate similar to Mexico's.

US marathon runner Dan Browne trains in a special high altitude chamber at the headquarters of sportswear company Nike. The chamber simulates conditions at high-altitude marathon locations around the world.

Altitude fact

Marathon runners need good supplies of oxygen from the air to perform well. At the Mexico City Olympics, the air was about 10 per cent less dense than at sea level. This meant it contained 10 per cent less oxygen. The top ten finishers in the marathon all ran more slowly than their previous personal best times. One Australian, Derek Clayton, ran *17* minutes slower.

The final countdown

Some marathon runners want to train hard right up to race day. But after weeks and months of demanding training, the body needs some recovery time. Opinions vary on when an athlete should start 'tapering' – or reducing the training load. Some coaches advise three days beforehand, others suggest as much as three weeks. During this period, any slightly damaged muscles can heal. An easier pre-race phase of training also allows for maximum **glycogen** build-up in the leg muscles.

The three 'R's of peak performance

An athlete aims to arrive at the marathon starting line feeling *R*ested, *R*efreshed and *R*eady-to-run. These are the three 'R's of peak performance. Runners have different ideas about how to achieve this state. Eating properly is vital (see page 32). But while some runners, like the UK's Eamonn Martin, enjoy a short, fast race a week before a marathon, others prefer to spend time just thinking about the marathon they will be running.

Yet even the most careful taper can go wrong. Fifteen days before the 1984 Olympic marathon, Portugal's Carlos Lopes was hit by a car while training. 'There goes the Olympics', thought Lopes as his elbow crashed through the car's windscreen. He need not have worried. He won the gold medal in a record time of 2:09:21!

Expos or exhibitions are staged before many big marathons. Competitors are advised not to trudge around the displays on the day before a race – it is much better for them to 'get horizontal' and rest!

Back | Forward | Stop | Refresh | Home | AutoFill | Print | Mail

Address: http://www.runningtimes.com/clinic/programs/marathonbasic.htm

	Mon	Tues*	Wed	Thurs**	Fri	Sat	Sun
Week 1	6	WO1	6	AT1	6	15	off
Week 2	6	WO2	8	AT2	6	18	off
Week 3	6	WO3	8	6	4	race (5K)	off
Week 4	6	12	8	AT3	6	20	off
Week 5	6	WO4	8	12	6	AT4	off
Week 6	6	WO5	8	6	4	race 10K	off
Week 7	6	12	8	AT5	6	23	off
Week 8	6	WO6	8	AT6	6	18	off
Week 9	6	WO7	8	12	off	AT7	off
Week 10	6	WO8	8	6	4	race 5K	off
Week 11	6	10	off	WO9	off	AT8	10
Week 12	off	WO10	off	6	off	3	Marathon

Tuesday (and one Thursday) Speed Workouts (WO):

Strides: You should do 6-8 times 100 yards at stride effort three times per week.

Warm Up: Warm up at least 15-20 minutes before a speed workout or race. Most of it should be easy but as the body warms up the pace can be increased so that when it is time to do the repetitions the body is ready. Jog 10-20 minutes after the completion of the repetitions to cool down.

AT = Anaerobic Threshold workouts. These workouts are often called LA (Lactic acid) runs or tempo runs and should be done at your anaerobic threshold. Magazine and much research reports this to be at 85% of maximum heart rate but the reality is that it varies considerably for individuals. Frank Shorter was reported to be able to run in the low 90%'s, for most of us it is probably between 77% and 85%. This is one of the numbers that is worth getting tested.

Internet marathon training programmes – like this one supplied by Runningtimes.com – advise athletes on how best to taper in the last days before a race.

Peters peters out!

The UK's Jim Peters was one of the all-time marathon greats. Between 1952 and 1954 he improved the world record from 2:25:39 to 2:17:39. But he followed such a punishing training programme – with no built-in taper – that he suffered problems as a result. At the 1952 Olympic Games and the 1954 Commonwealth Games, despite being the favourite to win both races, he broke down and failed to finish. Had he given himself some easier training days and tapered before races (like most marathon runners today) his career may have been even more glorious.

Common cold fact

Exercise is healthy and stops athletes from catching lots of everyday infections. But through final-phase overtraining, marathon runners' resistance can be lowered. In a survey, no fewer than 40 per cent of runners in a Los Angeles Marathon caught common colds in the two months before the race. Colds can be caught after all the effort of the race as well. London Marathon winner Eamonn Martin supplements his diet with vitamin C and zinc in an attempt to prevent colds.

Pre-race rituals

Every athlete today has his or her own way of going into a marathon. Once they have arrived safely at the race **venue**, runners spend more time on mental rather than physical forms of preparation. Most marathons are held in the morning, so a good night's rest beforehand helps. 'The important thing to remember about the last 24 hours,' writes Hal Higdon, 'is that nothing much you do on this day – except what you eat and drink – will have much effect on your race.'

BREAKFAST
*125g muesli/cereal/porridge
    with semi-skimmed milk
2 slices of wholemeal toast
1 piece of fruit – preferably a banana
1 glass of fruit juice*

SNACK
*1 wholemeal salad sandwich
50g mixed nuts and raisins
1 apple*

LUNCH
*1 baked potato with baked beans
1 glass of fruit juice*

SNACK
*small pasta salad (224g), with kidney beans,
    sweetcorn and salad vegetables
125g fresh fruit salad*

DINNER
*125g chicken/fish/shellfish
125g rice or potatoes
mixed salad
1 orange*

SNACK
*2 slices of wholemeal bread/toast
1 tablespoonful of honey
1 banana*

This list shows an athlete's food intake for a typical 'carbo-loading' day.

Fuelling up

'Fuelling up' can be tough for **elite** athletes. 'All that food and inactivity makes me irritable,' says Liz McColgan, 'and the thought of what lies ahead makes me anxious, so one way and another I'm not the most sociable of animals!'

'All that food', as Liz called it, is no exaggeration. In the days before a race many runners eat well to build up their **carbohydrate** reserves, thus storing vital supplies of muscle and liver **glycogen** (see page 16). This routine is called '**carbo-loading**'. It often comes to a peak with a 'pasta party', shared by a number of competitors on the eve of the race. But for days beforehand, runners will have been eating meals rich in carbohydrates (see typical examples above). They will have taken on board plenty of fluid too, to make sure they are well **hydrated** for the race.

Clearing the system

Finally, an athlete cannot afford to fuel up too close to the start of the race. The stomach needs time to digest food, before the bowels can then be cleared. It also takes about 30 minutes for liquids to travel from the mouth to the bladder. So unless runners intend to make toilet-stops in the race, it is sensible to stop drinking 30 minutes beforehand. (Last-minute liquid top-ups will probably be sweated out before they reach the bladder.) In the 1991 World Championships, American Steve Spence passed water three times but still managed to finish third!

Kit-bag checklist

The following items are always useful on the day of a big race:
• **Running numbers and pins to fix them to clothing**
• **Warm top, to be discarded at start of race**
• **Energy drink for last-minute carbo-loading**
• **Energy-bar or peanuts**
• **Plasters**
• **Vaseline**
• **Tape and bandages**
• **Sunscreen (if necessary)**
• **Gloves and hat (if necessary).**

The crowded starting grid at the 2003 London Marathon. With thousands of competitors, it can sometimes take 10 minutes for all the runners to get across the starting line. But thanks to the ChampionChip® (see page 25), everyone's true starting time can now be recorded.

The problem of pace

What is the best way to run a marathon? Clearly the distance is far too great to sprint all the way. But should you set off fast, step up the speed only later in the race, or simply stick to an even pace for the full 42.195 km? Some great champions of the past – such as Jim Peters and Frank Shorter – liked to outrun the opposition from the very start of a race. This 'early-surge' style is called front-running. The UK's Steve Jones was a famous recent front-runner. In 1985 he won the Chicago Marathon in a British record time of 2:07:13 – running the first half of the race in a blistering 1:01:43, the second in 1:05:30.

Fatuma Roba of Ethiopia has one of the most beautiful running actions. Spectators at the 1996 Olympic marathon at Atlanta, USA, had plenty of opportunity to admire it – she won gold after holding the lead for the entire second half of the race.

Run rabbit run

'All in all, I think it's no secret that even pacing works best.' That is the opinion of Nashville coach Robert Eslick, and many others nowadays agree. 'Level-pace' running ensures that runners do not 'blow up' in a race's early stages. By spreading their energy evenly, they perform to their peak.

How do athletes know if they are running to pace? In most modern big-city marathons (but not in international championships) pacemakers are employed to set a regular pace for the leading runners. Then, at around the halfway or even 32-km mark, these 'rabbits' retire – and the true race to the finish begins. Pacemakers can usefully reduce the air resistance on those behind; they can also allow the chasing pack to concentrate more on the rhythm of their running, and less on how fast they are going.

One of history's most famous pace-makers, Christopher Brasher (front), sets the pace for Roger Bannister (second) to run the first sub 4-minute mile in Oxford, 1954. Brasher later helped to found the London Mararthon.

Ronaldo's runaway record

Brazilian athlete Ronaldo da Costa was one of twelve children, including his own twin. In 1998 he shot to fame by winning the Berlin Marathon in a new world record time of 2:06:05 – beating Ethiopian Belayneh Dinsamo's previous world best by an amazing 45 seconds. He did it by running the race's first half in a steady 1:04:42, before tearing through the second half in 1:01:23. And he still had enough energy left at the finish to turn cartwheels in celebration of his victory!

Negative splits fact

Few athletes are naturally able to run a marathon's second half faster than the first. This is known as running 'negative splits', or 'reverse splits'; some people call it a 'back-to-front' approach to marathon running. One way of achieving negative splits is to treat the 32-km point as 'halfway' in terms of effort, then go for broke over the last 10 km.

Race strategy

Championship marathon running is not about speed alone. It also involves overcoming opposition. This opposition can come in the form of race-day conditions: all those challenges posed by the course or the weather. It also exists in the form of all the other competitors. Champion marathoners must prove not just that they are fast but that they are faster than anyone else on the day. To do this, they often have to outwit as well as outrun their closest rivals.

At the 1982 Boston Marathon Dick Beardsley (pictured left) felt exhausted after 21 miles. But by pretending that each of the last five miles was the very last mile of the race, he was able to maintain his pace to finish second.

High-performance principles

We have already seen that marathon running is like playing chess on your feet. Athletes have to be on constant guard against 'mind drift', especially in the race's gruelling later stages. By being alert, they can quickly adjust their race tactics to whatever is going on around them. But they also need a longer-term race strategy that they must try to stick to, no matter what happens on the day.

Every athlete has a highly personal strategy. There are certain principles, however, that most runners keep to. The first is to think of the race distance in stages. These could be 10 km sections, or the race could be broken up at the 10-mile, halfway and 20-mile points. It is easier to concentrate on completing shorter stages than on the enormous distance of 42.195 km. A second principle is to fight against the urge to accelerate – or 'race' – until the race's final stage, for this can lead to early burnout. A third principle is that after 26 km or so, the athlete should work really hard to 'focus in' on his or her performance. This is because it is much harder to concentrate as tiredness begins to set in.

At Helsinki in 1994, Martin Fiz, Diego Garcia and Alberto Juzdado of Spain worked together as a 'team' to win themselves the gold, silver and bronze medals in the European Championship Marathon. By taking it in turns to raise the pace over the last 11 km, they outran all the other athletes. Here they celebrate the success of their strategy.

Late start, early surge!

The USA's Joan Benoit did not excel at college athletics. She was 21 before she ran her first marathon in 1979. But between then and the 1984 US Olympic trial race she ran in ten, won five and set a world record of 2:22:43. Then, at the 1984 Olympics, her strategy was to take an early lead – and stay there. Surging to the front after just 14 minutes, she went on to become the first female Olympic marathon champion in a time of 2:24:52.

Making a break

Marathon runners must think on their feet during races. They have to react quickly to the tactics of others. They also have to make the vital decision on when to make their break and run for home. It could be halfway through the race; it could be on the last stretch. This depends partly on how the race has developed, and partly on the runner's personal preference for sprint-finishing or front-running.

Leaving the best till last

Some champion athletes have a knack of holding their best in reserve until they most need it. This is known as the art of 'controlled aggression'. At the 1988 Olympic marathon in Seoul, Gelindo Bordin of Italy came from behind in the last 3 km to win. Two years later at the Boston Marathon, he again held back his big push. This demanded a good deal of self-control, since a group of six African runners burned up the first half of the race in 1:02:01. But Bordin hung in there, almost a minute behind the leaders, until at 27 km he finally struck for home. Having made his break in his own good time, he won the race by an impressive 15-second margin.

Italy's Gelindo Bordin (left) won one of the closest Olympic marathons for years at Seoul, South Korea, in 1988. Briefly the four front-runners were all on the stadium track together. But Bordin sped away to win by a 15-second margin.

Leaving it too late

It can be dangerous, however, to let a rival run too far ahead. At the 1999 London Marathon, the race favourites – including Portugal's Antonio Pinto – chose not to keep up with the pace-making 'rabbits'. So they ran a slow first half of 1:04:55. But little-known Abdelkader El Mouaziz of Morocco stayed on the pace. By the time the last rabbit dropped out, after 27 km, El Mouaziz had a lead of almost 2 minutes. Pinto did not give chase until the 37-km mark. By then El Mouaziz was inevitably slowing down. But after building up such a lead by making his early break, he still finished the race a minute ahead of Pinto.

Spain's Abel Anton left it very late to win the 1997 World Championship Marathon in Athens, Greece. With just 300 metres of the race to go, he surged for glory with a devastating sprint finish. Here he tests how good his gold medal tastes after winning again in Seville, Spain, in 1999.

Brave Barcelona breakers

What happens when two athletes make their break at the same time? You get a brilliant showdown – especially during the final stages of an ultra-tough Olympic marathon. The course at Barcelona in 1992 ended with an awesome climb up to the Olympic stadium (see page 28). For 4 km before it, Japan's Koichi Morishita and Korea's Hwang Young-cho ran side by side. Then both decided to head for home. But whenever one surged ahead, the other caught up. Their cat-and-mouse game thrilled millions of TV viewers – until, 2 km from the stadium, Hwang finally sped away to victory.

After the race

'The three days after the race were the most miserable days of my life. Every bone ached. Every muscle ached. Even my fingernails ached!' This was the experience of a first-time marathoner in 1979 – and that was just the beginning. Full recovery after a marathon takes about six weeks. But after the race and in the following weeks, runners can take several steps to look after their bodies.

'The 27th mile'

'After the race,' says Liz McColgan, 'I get ice on the sorest parts of my body, take on more fluid [to **rehydrate**], eat and sip on another **carbo-load** drink, which very effectively replenishes lost energy and seems to make me less stiff the following morning. I soak in the bath and have a gentle massage to relax the muscles. The next day I find that it's good to start moving again, so I'll do a light jog, and then have a break to let my body completely recover.'

Few champion athletes would act differently, apart perhaps from the light jog. Just after the race, it is important to keep moving for 10 minutes or so; this helps to stop stiffness and soreness later. It is also important to wrap up, since runners lose heat fast once they stop racing. Most coaches also advise some simple stretching after strenuous exercise – a few short moves, just to maintain flexibility.

A gentle massage can be very helpful, especially 24 to 48 hours after the race – often the peak time for muscle soreness. At many major marathons there are massage tents with teams of trained massage therapists offering soothing rubdowns.

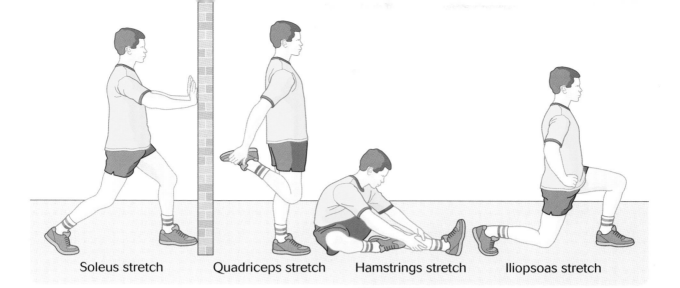

Soleus stretch   Quadriceps stretch   Hamstrings stretch   Iliopsoas stretch

Time to regroup

'Nature takes care of us,' writes Dr David L. Costill, a researcher into the effects of running 42.195 km on the human body. 'Time heals most of the damage done in the marathon.' By not running too hard, too fast or too soon after a big race, athletes can ease themselves back into their training programme and feel no harmful effects. This recovery period is also a chance to relax – and to rediscover that life is not just about marathon training and running!

Theses are some useful post-race stretches. However, beginners should seek advice from an expert about which exercises are right for them.

Many runners wrap themselves in tin foil after finishing a marathon – a good way to stop their bodies from losing heat too quickly.

Cooling down fact

It is bad for the body to start exercising suddenly, without warming up. It can also be harmful to stop exercising abruptly, without 'cooling down'. Simple stretches let hard-working blood vessels shut down gradually. Without these, athletes could suffer from a sudden drop in blood pressure, causing them to faint.

Being a champion marathon runner

Haile Gebrselassie grew up in poverty in Ethiopia. He developed his running style by racing 10 km to school every day. Then he went on to win four World Championship titles and two Olympic gold medals at 10,000m and 5000m. Many experts now call him the greatest distance runner of all time. 'Do you have anything left to prove?' he was asked in 2003. 'Oh yes', Gebrselassie said, still looking ahead: 'The marathon is the most important to me… The marathon, that would be good!' Even the great Gebrselassie thinks of a major marathon title as the top prize. For over a century, **elite** athletes worldwide have shared his vision.

A true test of character

The marathon is a true test of fitness, of racing skills and of sheer fighting spirit. You have now read about many champion marathoners, each with their own individual way of meeting the race's challenge. Athletics fans love to identify the personal styles of great runners and watch their true characters emerging over the huge distance. One of the most colourful long-distance-running characters of all time was Czech runner Emil Zátopek.

A champion marathon runner of the future? Ethiopia's Haile Gebrselassie (wearing number 10 here) sets out on the hard road to long-distance success.

A carpenter's son, Zátopek ran all around the local hills and forests as a child. Then he became a soldier and kept running, often in his army boots! When the 1952 Olympics began, Zátopek already held world records at 10,000m, 10 miles, 20 km and the 1-hour run. Few were surprised, therefore, when he won Olympic gold over 10,000m and 5000m. Indeed, many were delighted, for he was an extremely generous, witty, likeable man. But then he entered the marathon – never having run the distance of 42,195 km in his life!

An amazing victory

Unsure how to pace himself, he stuck alongside Jim Peters (see page 31), who had run the fastest marathon in history just weeks before. But at 15 km Peters began to flag, having set off way too fast. Zátopek – chatty as ever – asked him if the pace was fast enough. 'No', Peters replied (pretending he still felt fresh), 'it's too slow'. At that, Zátopek surged on – joking along the way with spectators and officials – to win the race in a new Olympic record time of 2:23:03.2.

Emil Zátopek grins as he wins the 1952 Olympic marathon. Usually he looked extremely pained as he ran. Asked why, he replied, 'I was not talented enough to run and smile at the same time!'

The huge crowd rose in awe. A Jamaican relay team carried him shoulder-high around the field. Spectators and athletes alike were saluting a very special runner. He had won the ultimate race in his own unique way. He – and they – now knew just what it meant to be a marathon champion.

Abebe Bikila from Ethiopia was the first black African ever to win an Olympic gold medal. In 1960 he won the marathon in Rome, Italy – running barefooted! To prove this was no fluke, he also won the next Olympic marathon in Tokyo, Japan – this time in shoes. On both occasions he broke the world record.

Marathon records and landmarks

Below is a selection of marathon records and landmarks achieved since the first modern Olympic marathon in 1896. When looking at the tables, it should be remembered that the official marathon distance of 26 miles 385 yards (42.195 km) was fixed only in 1924. The world records on page 45 were correct as of 1/12/03.

Key: OR = Olympic record, WR = world record.

Olympic marathon winners: men		
1896	Spiridon Louis (Greece)	2:58:50
1900	Michel Théato (France)	2:59:45
1904	Thomas Hicks (USA)	3:28:53
1908	John Hayes (USA)	2:55:18.4 OR
1912	Kenneth McArthur (South Africa)	2:36:54.8 OR
1920	Hannes Kolehmainen (Finland)	2:32.35.8 OR/WR
1924	Albin Stenroos (Finland)	2:41.22.6
1928	Boughèra El Ouafi (France)	2:32:57
1932	Juan Carlos Zabala (Argentina)	2:31:36 OR
1936	Sohn Kee-chung (Japan)	2:29:19.2 OR
1948	Delfo Cabrera (Argentina)	2:34:51.6
1952	Emil Zátopek (Czechoslovakia)	2:23:03.2 OR
1956	Alain Mimoun (France)	2:25:00
1960	Abebe Bikila (Ethiopia)	2:15:16.2 OR/WR
1964	Abebe Bikila (Ethiopia)	2:12:11.2 OR/WR
1968	Mamo Wolde (Ethiopia)	2:20:26.4
1972	Frank Shorter (USA)	2:12:19.8
1976	Waldemar Cierpinski (East Germany)	2:09:55 OR
1980	Waldemar Cierpinski (East Germany)	2:11:03
1984	Carlos Lopes (Portugal)	2:09:21 OR
1988	Gelindo Bordin (Italy)	2:10:32
1992	Hwang Young-cho (South Korea)	2:13:23
1996	Josiah Thugwane (South Africa)	2:12:36
2000	Gezahegne Abera (Ethiopia)	2:10.11

Olympic marathon winners: women		
1984	Joan Benoit (USA)	2:24:52 OR
1988	Rosa Mota (Portugal)	2:25:40
1992	Valentina Yegorova (Russia)	2:32:41
1996	Fatuma Roba (Ethiopia)	2:26:05
2000	Naoko Takahashi (Japan)	2:23:14 OR

World Athletics Championship winners: men

1983	Rob de Castella (Australia)	2:10:03
1987	Douglas Wakihiru (Kenya)	2:11:48
1991	Hiromi Taniguchi (Japan)	2:14:57
1993	Martin Plaatjes (South Africa)	2:13:57
1995	Martin Fiz (Spain)	2:11:41
1997	Abel Anton (Spain)	2:13:16
1999	Abel Anton (Spain)	2:13:36
2001	Gezahegne Abera (Ethiopia)	2:12:42
2003	Jaouad Gharib (Morocco)	2:08:31

World Athletics Championship winners: women

1983	Grete Waitz (Norway)	2:28:09
1987	Rosa Mota (Portugal)	2:25:17
1991	Wanda Panfil (Poland)	2:29:53
1993	Junko Asari (Japan)	2:30:03
1995	Manuela Machado (Portugal)	2:25:39
1997	Hiromi Suzuki (Japan)	2:29:48
1999	Song-Ok Jong (North Korea)	2:26:59
2001	Lidia Simon (Romania)	2:26:01
2003	Catherine Ndereba (Kenya)	2:23:55

Fastest times: men

World record	Paul Tergat (Kenya)	2:04:55	28/09/03
World debut	Evans Rutto (Kenya)	2.05.50	12/10/03
World under-20s	Li Zhuhong (China)	2.10.46	14/10/01
World 90–94 years (!)	Fauja Singh (UK)	5:40:02	28/09/03

Fastest times: women

World record	Paula Radcliffe (UK)	2:15:25	13/04/03
World debut	Paula Radcliffe (UK)	2:18:56	14/04/02
World under-20s	Liu Min (China)	2:23:37	14/10/01
World 90–94 years (!)	Mavis Lindgren (USA)	8:53:08	28/09/97

Repeat record-breakers fact

Only four men and seven women have followed one marathon world record with another. One of the greatest repeat record-breakers was Jim Peters of the UK, who set four world records between 1952 and 1954, while Ethiopia's Abebe Bikila, Australia's Derek Clayton and the USA's Khalid Khannouchi have each set two world records for the event. In the women's marathon, Norway's Grete Waitz set four world records in a row between 1978 and 1983 (though the last one stood just for one day!)

Glossary

Achilles tendons
fibres linking calf muscles to the heel

aerobic
using oxygen to produce energy

amateur
competing without being paid to
do so

calorie
the unit of a food's energy value

carbohydrates
energy-producing elements in food,
for example starch and glucose

carbo-load/carbo-loading
eating meals or drinks rich in
carbohydrates before a race

circulatory system
the way blood flows or circulates
around the body

coronary arteries
tubes that carry blood away from the
heart to the rest of the body

elite
top, high-achieving

fibres
tiny, thread-like connecting parts of
the body

glycogen
a substance in the body that powers
the liver and muscles

guinea
an old kind of British money, worth
just over £1

humid
warm and damp

hydrated
having enough water in the body for
it to function properly

labourer
a low-paid workman

mileage
the number of miles a person runs
(daily, weekly, etc.)

nutritionists
experts on healthy eating

professional
being paid to compete

protein
an essential health-giving element in
certain foods

qualifying time
a time under which an athlete must
already have run one marathon before
being allowed to compete in another

rehabilitation
getting the body back to normal

rehydrate
take on water again after losing it
from the body during a race

speedwork
fast-paced training sessions

spina bifida
a problem of the spine which can
result in a person's lower limbs being
paralysed

sponsored runners
runners who are paid sums of money
by firms or individuals for competing
in a race; this money can then be
given to charity

steeplechase
a race in which athletes must jump
over hurdles and water barriers

venue
a place where a race is held

Resources

Further reading

Marathon Manual, Cathy Shipton with Liz McColgan (Thorsons, 1997)

Marathon Running – From Beginner to Elite, Richard Nerurkar (A & C Black, 2000)

Marathon – The Ultimate Training Guide, Hal Higdon (Rodale, 1999)

All three of the above books give advice to the first-time runner as well as looking at the approaches taken by great marathon champions of the past.

Great Olympic Moments, Haydn Middleton (Heinemann Library, 1999)

Some outstanding feats from the glorious history of the Games.

Running Within, Jerry Lynch and Warren Scott (Human Kinetics, 1999)

A guide to mastering the body-mind-spirit connection for ultimate training and racing.

The Complete Book of the Olympics, David Wallechinsky (Aurum Press, 2000)

Facts and figures on every Olympic event since 1896.

The Olympic Marathon – the History and Drama of Sport's Most Challenging Event, David E. Martin and Roger W. H. Gynn (Human Kinetics, 2000)

A look at the history of the Olympic marathon over the years.

Websites

http://www.runnersworld.com/ – an up-to-the-minute site on every aspect of running.

http://www.marathonguide.com/ – this website provides information on every aspect of marathoning, past and present.

http://www.iaaf.org – the website of the International Association of Athletics Federations (IAAF), the world governing body for all track and field (athletic) events, including the marathon.

http://www.olympic.org – the home page of the International Olympic movement.

Disclaimer

Index

Titles in the *Making of a Champion* series include:

Hardback   0 431 18924 2

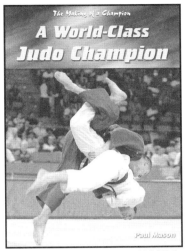

Hardback   0 431 18925 0

Hardback   0 431 18923 4

Hardback   0 431 18926 9

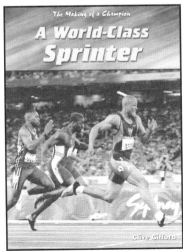

Hardback   0 431 18921 8

Hardback   0 431 18922 6

Find out about the other Heinemann Library titles on our website www.heinemann.co.uk/library